LU & CLANCY'S
CRIME
SCIENCE

written by **Louise Dickson**

illustrated by **Pat Cupples**

Kids Can Press

OCT 2 8 1999

Curr
HV
8073.8
D48
1999

Text copyright © 1999 by Louise Dickson
Illustrations copyright © 1999 by Patricia Cupples

All rights reserved. No part of this publication may be
reproduced, stored in a retrieval system or transmitted,
in any form or by any means, without the prior
written permission of Kids Can Press Ltd. or, in case
of photocopying or other reprographic copying, a
license from CANCOPY (Canadian Copyright
Licensing Agency), 1 Yonge Street, Suite 1900,
Toronto, ON, M5E 1E5.

Neither the Publisher nor the Author shall be liable
for any damage which may be caused or sustained as
a result of conducting any of the activities in this
book without specifically following instructions,
conducting the activities without proper supervision,
or ignoring the cautions contained in the book.

Kids Can Press acknowledges the financial support of
the Ontario Arts Council, the Canada Council for the
Arts and the Department of Cultural Heritage.

Published in Canada by   Published in the U.S. by
Kids Can Press Ltd.   Kids Can Press Ltd.
29 Birch Avenue   85 River Rock Drive, Suite 202
Toronto, ON M4V 1E2   Buffalo, NY 14207

Edited by Valerie Wyatt
Designed by Julia Naimska
Printed in Hong Kong by Wing King Tong
Company Limited

CM PA 99 0 9 8 7 6 5 4 3 2 1

Canadian Cataloguing in Publication Data

Dickson, Louise, 1959 –
        Lu & Clancy's crime science

(Lu & Clancy)
ISBN 1-55074-552-2

1. Criminal investigation – Juvenile literature.
2. Forensic sciences – Juvenile literature. I. Cupples,
Patricia. II. Title. III. Title: Lu and Clancy's crime
science. IV. Series

HV8073.8.D48   1999   j363.25   C99-930314-7

For Sarah and Tess,
Gavan and Vivian,
Liam and Kira,
with love — LD

For Sara,
Katy and John,
with love — PC

Kids Can Press is a Nelvana company

Contents

Rambles
24 Puppycoat Lane
Barkerville

Doggone Puppies!

All was quiet in the tree house of Lu and Clancy, dog detectives. Lu was curled up on the couch dozing. Clancy had his nose buried in a newspaper. He was shaking his head over a story about dognappings in Barkerville when …

"Help! Help!"

Clancy dropped the newspaper. Lu fell off the couch. Both detectives ran to the window and stuck their heads out. Dottie, their next-door neighbor, was running in circles at the bottom of the tree.

"What's wrong?" Lu shouted down.

"My puppies are missing!" Dottie whined. "I just went outside for a minute. And when I went back in — they were gone!"

Lu and Clancy scampered down to the ground. Lu patted Dottie on the back. "Don't worry, Dottie. We'll find them."

"We'll need a forensic kit to gather evidence," said Clancy.

"Forensic — as in crime?" asked Dottie.

Clancy nodded. "The puppies may have been dognapped."

"Dognapped?" Dottie's eyes rolled back and she fainted dead away.

An Eye for Crime

As soon as Dottie recovered from her fainting spell, Lu and Clancy started asking her questions.

"What time did you notice the puppies were gone?"

"Did you see anyone else around?"

"What were the puppies wearing?"

"Did you notice anything suspicious?"

Dottie's head swung back and forth between the two dogs. "I can't remember!" she wailed. "The only thing I noticed was that the window was open. And there were dog-biscuit crumbs on the windowsill."

"Stay here in case the puppies turn up, Dottie," said Lu. Then, like highly trained police dogs, she and Clancy put their noses to the ground and followed the trail of crumbs.

How it works

How much would you remember if a crime was committed? Here's your chance to find out. Can you answer these questions about what was happening in the picture on pages 4 and 5? Don't turn back to look — just write down your answers, then check page 40 to find out how you scored.

- How many Dalmatian puppies are there?
- Where are they?
- Who are they following?
- What is the name of the newspaper?

- What shape are the dog biscuits?
- What time is it?
- What date is it?
- Are the puppies wearing anything special?

Fingering the Suspec

Lu and Clancy followed the trail of crumbs to the goldfish pond.

Lu circled the fishpond, sniffing furiously. "Something fishy is going on," she said. "I've lost the trail."

"You mean something fishy *has* gone on." Clancy pointed to a mishmash of wet paw prints.

Lu raised her nose and sniffed again. "Wait — I've picked up the scent. It's coming from that bush."

Clancy parted the branches and saw a fishing net. He peered closely at the handle. "Fingerprints! Our first clue."

Lu snapped on a pair of rubber gloves. "Better lift them as evidence."

How it works

Fingerprints are unique. Each person's are different. Detectives like to find fingerprints because the prints can help identify suspects. Scientists have classified fingerprints into eight different types (see page 40). Try lifting some fingerprints and see which type they are.

You'll need:
- cocoa
- a small paintbrush
- clear sticky tape
- white paper

1. If you can't find a nice clear print, make your own. Rub your fingers through your hair or along the side of your nose to make your fingertips oily. Press one finger at a time onto a clean drinking glass.

2. Sprinkle cocoa lightly over the fingerprints.

3. Gently brush off the loose cocoa powder with the paintbrush. You should be able to see the fingerprints.

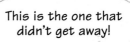

This is the one that didn't get away!

4. Carefully place a piece of tape over one fingerprint, then gently lift the tape off. The fingerprint pattern will be captured on the tape.

5. Stick the piece of tape onto the paper.

Spilled Milk

YEEOOOOWL!!

Lu pricked up her ears. "Sounds like a cat problem."

The yowling was coming from Kitty's. Empty milk bottles were scattered all over her porch.

"My breakfast, lunch and dinner! Gone!" she howled.

How it works

Like fingerprints, lip prints are unique. Each pair of lips has different lines, wrinkles and grooves. Here's how to collect lip prints and see for yourself.

You'll need:
- lipstick
- white paper
- clear sticky tape

1. Carefully cover your lips with lipstick.

2. Fold the piece of paper in half and place it between your lips. Press your lips to the paper.

"Now now, Kitty. No use crying over spilled milk," said Clancy.

Lu carefully picked up one of the empty bottles and examined it. "Aha! Fingers aren't the only things that leave prints." She pointed to a smudge on the bottle. "A lip print!"

"Collect that print and bag it, Lu." Clancy turned to the cat. "We'll do our best to track down the thief."

3. Remove the paper carefully, without smudging the lipstick. Look at the lip lines you've left.

4. To lift a lipstick print from a glass, carefully place a piece of clear sticky tape over the lip mark, then gently lift the tape off. The lip pattern should stick to the tape. Stick the tape onto a sheet of white paper.

Look what the dognapper left behind. We're going to lick this case.

A Handsome Ransom

Lu and Clancy were heading back to their tree house when …

"Clancy! Luuu!" Dottie ran up and handed them a note.

I've got the puppies. To keep them healthy, please leave a box of liver-flavored Doggy Num-Nums in the tunnel behind the fire hall. Thank you. P.S. Hurry up! They're hungry!

Was this a ransom note? Clancy was puzzled. The newspaper said the dognappers demanded money. But this dognapper just wanted food.

"Please and thank you," read Lu. "Our dognapper has manners — and a taste for liver."

"That's not all the note can tell us." Clancy turned to Dottie. "While you buy the dog biscuits, we'll test the ink in the note."

How it works

When police find a note at the scene of a crime, they analyze the ink and try to match it to the pen (and person) that wrote it. Different brands of pens leave different ink patterns on paper. Here's how to analyze pen ink.

You'll need:
- a water-soluble black felt-tip pen
- a strip of paper coffee filter about 2.5 cm x 10 cm (1 in. x 4 in.)
- sticky tape
- a drinking glass

1. Use the pen to scribble some ink about 1 cm (½ in.) from one end of the paper strip. The scribble should be dark and about the size of your baby fingernail. Pretend this is ink from a ransom note.

2. Tape the strip to the pen so that the scribbled end is hanging down.

3. Rest the pen across a drinking glass partly filled with water. The strip should just touch the water. The water will gradually crawl up the strip, taking the ink with it. Remove the strip and let it dry. Each kind of pen makes its own pattern.

This note spells trouble for our dognapper.

leave the tunnel hungry!

Grimestoppers

Lu and Clancy were on their way to deliver the ransom biscuits when they met Petey Pooch.

"Totally bad news, man. Someone stole my wheels."

"Your wheels?" asked Clancy.

"Yeah, man. My skateboard's gone."

"But the evidence isn't." Lu pointed to a footprint in the mud.

Clancy bent down to get a closer look. "Hmmmm. I think I saw this footprint on Kitty's porch."

"You know who took my skateboard?" asked Petey.

"Nope, but we're going to find out. Come on, Lu. Let's make a cast of this footprint."

How it works

Detectives make casts of footprints found at the scene of a crime. Footprints can help to identify the owner. For example, a pebble or a thumbtack caught in the treads leaves a distinctive mark. Worn parts might tell how the person walks. Some people wear down the outside of their shoes, others the inside.

You'll need:
- scissors
- an empty shoe box
- petroleum jelly
- plaster of paris (available at a hardware store)
- newspaper
- a small paintbrush

1. Cut out the bottom of the shoe box to make a frame. Grease the sides of the frame with petroleum jelly.

2. Look for a clear footprint in the dirt outside, or make one yourself by pressing the sole of your running shoe into soft soil. Place the shoe-box frame around the footprint.

3. Follow the directions on the plaster of paris package and mix up about 500 mL (2 c.) of plaster of paris in a disposable container.

4. Pour the wet plaster into the frame to cover the footprint. Let it harden. This will take about 20 to 30 minutes.

5. Peel off the frame. Carefully lift the hardened plaster and bring it inside. Place it on a newspaper and let it dry overnight.

6. When the plaster is dry, use the paintbrush to brush the soil off the cast. Can you see the footprint?

A Clean Getaway

"Clancy! Lu!"

Oh no, thought Clancy, not another interruption. They *had* to get the ransom biscuits to the tunnel.

But Madge wasn't letting them by. "Look at this mess. Those dogs raced through here like greyhounds after a rabbit. Now I'm going to have to wash everything all over again."

How it works

The length of someone's foot is usually about 15 percent of his or her height. Knowing this, detectives can calculate the height of a suspect from a shoe print. Here's how to do it.

You'll need:
- a measuring tape
- a pencil and paper
- a calculator

Lu stared at a footprint on a pillowcase. "Hmmmm. The dognapper is shorter than I thought."

"How do you know?" asked Madge.

"You can tell someone's height by the length of his or her foot." She reached for her measuring tape. "I'll show you."

1. Measure the length of someone's foot.

2. Divide this number by 15 and multiply by 100. For example, if the footprint is 18 cm (7 in.) long, divide this number by 15 and multiply by 100. The answer is 120 cm (47 in.).

Lasting Impressions

Lu and Clancy were worried. "Those puppies must be getting awfully hungry," said Lu, as they hurried to deliver the ransom.

"The fire hall is just a block away," Clancy was saying, when he was nearly knocked over by Big Ben the butcher.

"Some rascals ran off with my pies and sausages," Big Ben growled and pointed down the street. "They went thataway."

Clancy took off in hot pursuit.

Lu poked her head through the door of the butcher shop. The place looked like a dog's breakfast. Plates were broken. Food was scattered.

She stooped down and picked up a meat pie. "Bite marks," she explained to Big Ben. "Mind if I take this as evidence?"

How it works

Bite marks are unique. An impression made by someone's teeth can show if the person has an overbite, an underbite or crooked or missing teeth. What does your bite say?

You'll need:
• scissors
• a Styrofoam plate

1. Cut the Styrofoam plate into six equal pie-shaped pieces.

2. Stack the six pie-shaped pieces one on top of another. Cut off the pointed ends.

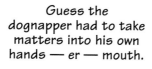

3. Put the wedges in your mouth and bite down hard. The top wedge has the impression of your top teeth. The bottom wedge has the impression of your bottom teeth.

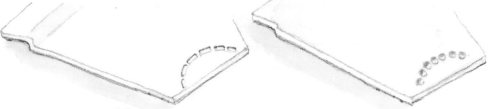

4. Compare your top and bottom teeth with the impressions they made. Count them. Look at their shapes. Notice which ones are crooked and where there are gaps.

Guess the dognapper had to take matters into his own hands — er — mouth.

The Chase

Ahead of him, Clancy saw a bicycle disappearing around a corner. He pushed his short legs to carry him faster.

Over a hedge he went, down a slide, under a swing and through Madge's clean sheets. Then the bicycle vanished. Clancy screeched to a halt by a gap in a fence. Something tickled his nose. He brushed away a tuft of brown hair. There was more on the fence. Aha!

How it works

Forensic scientists examine a hair sample and compare it with hair taken from a suspect. From a single strand of hair, scientists can tell the age, sex and race of the person it came from. You can collect hair samples, too.

You'll need:
- clear sticky tape
- strands of hair from a few friends
- fur from a few pets
- small pieces of paper or index cards
- a microscope or magnifying glass

1. Use the tape to stick each strand of hair or fur to a piece of paper.

2. Write the name of the person or pet on the back of the paper.

He dashed through the fence just in time to see a bicycle speeding away down a muddy track.

"Doggone it," he wheezed as the bicycle disappeared from sight.

He returned to the gap in the fence. Lu arrived just as he was bagging the hair. "More evidence," he said, holding the bag out to her.

3. Look at your samples through the microscope or magnifier.

- How long is the hair?
- How thick is the hair?
- Is it curly or straight?
- What color is it?
- Is it the same color all the way along the strand?
- Is it coarse or smooth?
- Is it dull or shiny?

Here are some tips to help you if you find hair at a crime scene:

- Men's hair is thicker than women's.
- Dyed hair is dull.
- Undyed hair is shiny.
- Dog fur is coarse.
- Cat fur is smooth.

Back on Track

While Clancy was studying the hair sample, Lu sniffed around. "They left more than hair behind." She pointed to a bicycle track.

Clancy let out a yip of excitement. "Come on — we'll follow the track. It'll lead us right to them." He set off, with Lu behind him. But the muddy track ended at the pavement.

"Drat," said Clancy. "We almost had them."

"Let's take a photo of the tire track as evidence. Maybe we can find a tire that matches it."

Clancy grabbed his camera and — click! Seconds later, a picture emerged, and the two dogs set off to check out some bicycle tires.

How it works

Detectives take photographs of tire tracks at a crime scene, then try to match the tracks with the car or bicycle of a suspect. Here's how to collect a tire print from a bicycle.

You'll need:
• kitchen cooking oil in a spray can
• cocoa
• a small paintbrush
• clear sticky tape wider than the tire you will be testing
• a big piece of white paper

1. Spray about half of the bicycle's front tire with cooking oil. Find a clean patch of pavement. Roll the sprayed part of the wheel across the pavement.

2. Lightly sprinkle cocoa over the tire track.

3. Gently brush off the loose cocoa powder with the paintbrush. You should be able to see the tire track.

4. Carefully place a piece of tape over the tire track, then gently lift the tape off. The tire pattern should be captured on the tape.

So this is how you track a thief!

5. Stick the piece of tape onto the white paper.

The Write Stuff

Clancy and Lu compared bike tires with their photo.

"Too knobbly," sighed Clancy.

"Too narrow," sighed Lu.

"Clancy! Luuu!" Dottie bounded up with another pink note.

"Urgent," Clancy read. "The puppies are very hungry. Please bring the ransom now! Thank you."

Lu pointed to the bite taken out of the ransom note. "Those puppies *must* be hungry."

"Let's analyze the handwriting," said Clancy.

How it works

Handwriting experts analyze handwritten documents, such as notes passed to bank tellers by robbers, forged documents and even ransom notes. Then police compare the writing to a sample supplied by a suspect. Here's how to analyze handwriting.

You'll need:
• a pen and paper
• tracing paper
• a ruler

First, compare the *heights* of the letters and the *patterns* they form:

1. Write any word on a piece of paper. Put a piece of tracing paper over it.

2. Mark a dot on the tracing paper at the high point of each letter.

3. Use the ruler to join the dots.

4. Ask someone else to write the same word. Repeat steps 2 and 3. Do their lines look the same as yours?

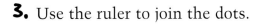

Now compare the *slant* of the letters:

5. Put a new piece of tracing paper over the word you wrote in step 1.

6. Use the ruler to make a line through each letter. The line you draw should have the same slant as the letter.

7. Ask someone else to write the same word and see how their letters slant.

Now all we need is a sample from our suspect.

Impressive Evidence

"Psst, Lu. Do you see what I see?"

The two dogs were racing to deliver the ransom biscuits when something stopped them dead in their tracks. A big red bike was leaning against a house. Lu quickly made a print of its front tire and compared it to the photo of the getaway bicycle track. "It's a match!"

The door to the house was ajar. "I wonder what else we'll find in here." Clancy poked his head in.

How it works

When you write on a pad of paper, your pen or pencil makes an impression on the paper underneath. Paper can provide important evidence for detectives. As they search a house, they check the blank page of a pad of paper for clues, such as a phone number. Here's how to make the invisible visible.

You'll need:
- a ballpoint pen
- a pad of paper
- a sharp lead pencil

The house was a wreck. Dishes were broken, chairs tipped over, socks and underwear scattered everywhere. There were puppy tracks on the walls, even on the ceiling. On the floor was a pad of pink paper that looked suspiciously like the ransom notes.

Clancy peered at it. "No clues here. It's blank."

"Take a second look. There's more here than meets the eye." And Lu showed him how to find a note on a blank piece of paper.

Im-press-ive!

1. Pressing hard with your ballpoint pen, write a pretend ransom note or secret message on the top page of the pad of paper.

2. Remove the second page and hold it up to the light. Can you read your message?

3. Lightly shade over the page with the pencil.

Burning Clues

Clancy wriggled with excitement. "Whoever lives here definitely wrote the ransom notes! Let's use the biscuits to set a trap!"

"Wait a minute, Clancy. The dognapper could be dangerous. We need to find out more about him."

The two detectives knew exactly where to look — the garbage.

Clancy reached into the garbage can and pulled out a foil plate that smelled of meat pie, a torn sheet, an empty milk bottle, the skeleton of a goldfish and a broken skateboard.

Lu checked the fireplace and found a book with a scorched cover. "How to Make Friends: A Guide for Lonely Dogs," she read.

Then she found an envelope. It was crumpled and burned, as if someone has been trying to destroy evidence. "Look! — this envelope will tell us the name of our dognapper!"

How it works

When detectives find burned paper during an investigation, they take it back to the crime lab and float it in a mixture of glycerin and water. This mixture softens the paper so that it can be flattened. Because most ballpoint-pen inks won't fade in a fire, the message can often be read. To restore a burned document, ask an adult to help you.

You'll need:

- a ballpoint pen and paper
- a metal pot
- matches
- tongs
- a cookie sheet
- 125 mL ($\frac{1}{2}$ c.) glycerin
- 375 mL (1 $\frac{1}{2}$ c.) water
- a spray bottle

1. Write a message on the paper using the ballpoint pen. Crumple the paper into a ball and put it in the pot. Ask an adult to light it on fire. **Warning:** Do not do this without an adult's help.

2. Let the paper partially burn, then blow it out. When the paper is cool, use tongs to put it on the cookie sheet.

3. Mix the glycerin and water together and pour the mixture into the spray bottle. Spray the paper until it is completely wet.

4. Carefully flatten the paper and see if you can read the message.

Your rambling days are over, Rambles.

Rambles
24 Puppycoat Lane
Barkerville

Whodunit?

Is Rambles the dognapper? Here is the evidence Lu and Clancy collected from Rambles' house. What do you think?

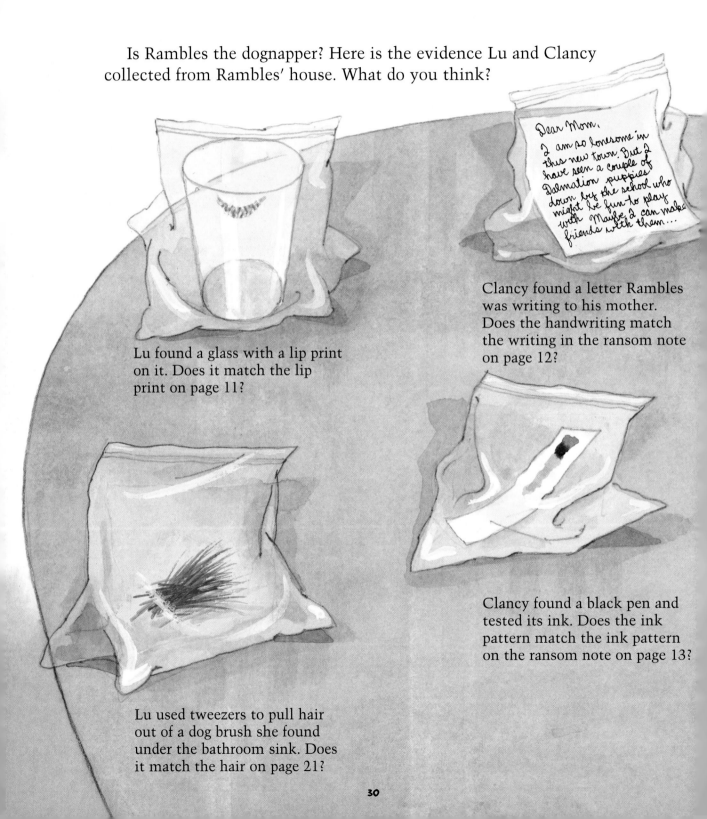

Dear Mom,
I am so lonesome in this new town. But I have seen a couple of Dalmation puppies down by the school who might be fun to play with. Maybe I can make friends with them...

Lu found a glass with a lip print on it. Does it match the lip print on page 11?

Clancy found a letter Rambles was writing to his mother. Does the handwriting match the writing in the ransom note on page 12?

Clancy found a black pen and tested its ink. Does the ink pattern match the ink pattern on the ransom note on page 13?

Lu used tweezers to pull hair out of a dog brush she found under the bathroom sink. Does it match the hair on page 21?

I think we can prove that Rambles did it.

Maybe ... but I'd sure like to check his fingerprints.

Lu pulled a sneaker out from under the bed. Does its tread match the footprint on page 14?

Clancy found an old piece of cheese in the fridge with a huge bite taken out of it. Do the bite marks match the bite marks in the meat pie on page 19?

Closing the Case

Clancy and Lu crept to the edge of the tunnel and quietly stuffed the ransom biscuits inside.

They heard the box being torn open, then scuffling, munching, crunching and licking. They waited, but no one came out. They waited some more. Then they waited a while longer.

"I'm going in, Lu."

"I'm coming with you."

The tunnel was very dark. As their eyes got used to the dimness, Clancy and Lu made out the shapes of three sleeping dogs.

Quickly Clancy took Rambles' fingerprints — the last piece of evidence.

"He's our dognapper, all right," he said, shaking the dog awake.

Rambles woke up and yelped, "I only wanted to make friends!"

His howling woke the puppies. One licked Rambles' nose, while the other nibbled his ear.

"We've solved the case, Clancy," said Lu. "And Rambles has made some new friends."

How it works

All criminals are fingerprinted and their prints are kept on file. When police lift a suspicious fingerprint, they look through their files to find a matching print.

You'll need:
- a pencil
- white paper
- clear sticky tape

1. Rub the pencil point back and forth on the paper until you have a small dark area of pencil-lead dust.

2. Rub each finger into the blackened area.

3. Press each finger onto the sticky side of a piece of tape.

4. Tape each piece of tape onto another piece of white paper.

Now It's Your Turn

The next morning the newspaper arrived with a thud at the base of the tree house. Clancy scooted down the ladder and picked it up. Another dognapping! Only this time it was for real.

Check out the evidence and see if you can help Lu and Clancy solve this case.

Dognappers strike again

Three young dachshunds disappeared from Sausage Row School yard late Monday afternoon. They may be the latest victims in a series of dognappings that have swept Barkerville over the past few months.

Yesterday, dog detectives Lu and Clancy of Two Dogs Inc. reunited Dottie Delaney with her pups. That dognapping, however, turned out to be nothing more than a young mutt's misguided attempt to make new friends.

Detective Doberman of the Barkerville Police Force said the disappearance of the dachshunds is far more sinister. Once again the dognappers are demanding a huge ransom for each puppy.

Detective Doberman has asked Lu and Clancy to assist in the investigation.

Police are warning parents to keep an eye on their puppies at all times until the dognappers are safely behind bars.

The Witness

Detective Doberman drove the two detectives to the school yard where the puppies had disappeared.

On the way, Lu asked, "Any eyewitnesses?"

"The gardener, Boris, saw the dognappers running away. He's ready to give a full statement."

When they arrived at the school, Lu and Clancy talked to Boris.

"I was planting some flowers about 4:30 p.m. when I heard barking in the playground. It wasn't happy barking. It sounded like trouble.

"I dropped my trowel and ran around to the playground, but there was no one there. Suddenly, out of the corner of my eye, I saw one dog — or was it two? — I can't remember, it happened so fast — pedaling off on a bicycle in a flash of red and a blur of brown and white.

"I heard squealing coming from a burlap sack in the basket of the bicycle. Then I found the ransom note, and I called the police right away."

"Well done, Boris. You did the right thing," said Clancy.

The Evidence

Here is the evidence that Lu and Clancy found at the crime scene. Check it out carefully, then turn the page to meet the suspects.

The Suspects

Read Detective Doberman's notes on each suspect to see if anything about them matches the clues on pages 36-37.

Cunning Clyde

○ Has a reputation for raiding garbage cans.
○ Sneaky smile -- a mouthful of straight, sharp teeth.
  Found carrying a skateboard.
○ Handwriting sample:

2 hate fleas.

Sly Scottie

○ An incurable car chaser.
  Never stops talking about $.
○ Found in-line skating.
  Definite overbite.
  Handwriting sample:

○ *I hate fleas.*

Bold Babe

Says she hates puppies.
Led police in a high-speed chase
○ on a 10-speed.
Fanglike overbite.
Handwriting sample:

○ *I hate fleas.*

Mean Matt

Lean and mean.
Claims he never learned to ride
○ a bicycle.
Missing his two front teeth.
Handwriting sample:

○ *I hate fleas.*

Whodunit? Use the evidence on pages 36 and 37 to find out, then turn to page 40 to see if you are right.

Answers

page 7
An Eye for Crime

If you scored:	It means:
0-2	Take another peek.
3-4	You're getting an eye for crime.
5-6	You're an eagle-eyed beagle.
7-8	You're one hot dog detective.

pages 34-39
Now It's Your Turn

To figure it out, make a chart like the one below and put **Yes** or **No** or **?** for each question. The two suspects with the most **Yes** answers are the dognappers (answer below).

	Clyde	Scottie	Babe	Matt
Brown or white hair?				
Wearing something red?				
Owns a bicycle?				
Has an overbite?				
Handwriting matches ransom note?				

Answer:

The dognappers are Scottie and Babe.

Common Fingerprint Patterns

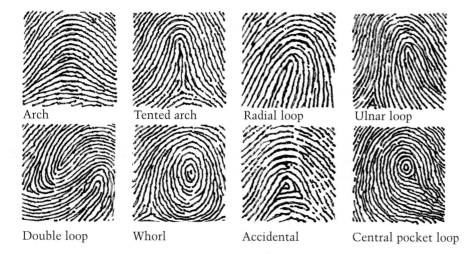

Arch	Tented arch	Radial loop	Ulnar loop
Double loop	Whorl	Accidental	Central pocket loop